REDEFINED

30 Days to Your True Identity

ANDREA LEBEAU

Cover photo:
Andrea LeBeau

ISBN-13: 978-1722106072
ISBN-10: 1722106077

FOREWORD

Oh, hey, girl! If you're picking up this book, I want you to take a deep breath. Breathe in truth, breathe out lies. I think for many of us, we do the opposite. We accept and let the lies settle deep within us, while the truth of who we are is drowned by those lies. We let the words of friends and family, the images we see on TV and social media, and the stereotypes floating around take root and begin to change our hearts, our minds, our thoughts, and ultimately, our belief in ourselves.

Over the next 30 days, I want to walk you through releasing the lies you believe about yourself and replacing them with the truth that is found in God's Word. I'm going to make you say things out loud and stretch you out of your comfort zone, but hear me when I say it's because I LOVE YOU SO MUCH. I do not want you walking around believing you are anything less than the daughter of the Most High King! You are His chosen and precious one, and to forget that, is a detriment to you and to the world that so desperately needs you to be you.

This topic is so important to me because of what God did to change my heart. I spent too many years walking around, believing that I wasn't enough while being way too much, too loud, too quiet, too hyper, too subdued, too extroverted, too introverted, too negative, too positive, too fat, too skinny, too anxious, too depressed, too mean, too nice, too confident, too uncertain, too strong, too weak, too stoic, too emotional. I could fill the first chapter with all of my "toos."

It was too much to bear and too much to sort through. Without God stepping in, I don't know where I'd be today. That thought is terrifying for two reasons: my future could have been nonexistent, and you could be feeling the exact same way I felt. Step outside of yourself for a second and imagine a sea of women all feeling the same "toos" you feel everyday. What an inferior, defeated, self-conscious group it is. When you don't release the lies and replace them with truth, you are walking around each day with no power or authority or confidence in who your Creator handcrafted you to be.

Words don't define you. Your sins don't define you. Circumstances don't define you. So, leave those definitions on this page, and let's redefine you as God's perfect, amazing, talented, beautiful, very good princess of the King. I love you too much to let you stay here with your "toos."

xoxo,

day one

YOU ARE NEW

As a child, I was confident. I liked New Kids on the Block, I had crimped hair and neon tights, I hated strawberry Nestle Quik after an incident with my little sister on the floor of a Ralph's grocery store, I was smarter than my mother, and I had never met a stranger. I could make friends with anyone based on commonalities. I was witty, I was joyful, and I was confident. Somewhere between first grade and fifth grade, my confidence paled. I still knew who I was, but the time I had spent in school had given me a few bumps and bruises from other snotty kids who were also smarter than their mothers.

I went on to high school and wasn't unpopular, but also not terribly popular. I had a dorky group of girlfriends who loved 'NSYNC almost as much as I did, and we spent countless sleepovers discussing boys. Our friendship spanned the course of high school, and we stuck like glue to each other. We dated boys and got dumped by boys, we failed quizzes, we even did each other's chores during overnights. We acted as a fortress for each other when the outside world made us feel inferior.

Along the way, I was met with the real world outside of that small, Christian school. Our school had all the same issues a public school had, but on a less terrifying scale. My polo shirts were shockingly uncool outside the carpeted walls of our school. I had dreams and goals that were shot down, I started a bout with an eating disorder, I went through a football-helmet-hair phase, I worked a job at a pretzel shop, my parents separated, I had some weird Biblical interpretations spoken into my life, and a million other things that shaped me into a young adult.

Taking all of the bumps and bruises into my early twenties with a less-than-solid foundation in Christ, I attempted to wing it. I adopted an attitude of protection when I stepped foot into a church, which was every week being that my new husband now worked full-time for our church. I made grocery lists in my head as the worship team played so as not to catch the feels. God was perfectly confined in a box so that His ugly wrath and this disdain He, clearly, felt for me weren't able to permeate my very walled-off heart.

At 25, we were ready to start a family, but my body had other plans. I miscarried twice in one year, and let the feelings of utter failure wash over me. I was designed to make and carry babies, and my body was actively working against me to make that happen. Hit after hit, my identity crumbled. I screamed at my ceiling, willing God to yell back at me that He wasn't leaving me in the wilderness, but sadly, my ceiling was silent.

When I got pregnant the first time, my due date was December 8, 2009. On December 8, 2009, I took a pregnancy test and found that I was pregnant. I delivered a 7 pound, 4 ounce beautiful, gray, alien baby girl on August 11, 2010.

Fast forward two years, I am pregnant again, only to miscarry and fall into the depths of anxiety. I'm not talking a little shortness of breath and sweaty pits, I am talking about full-blown, can't leave the house, every twitch makes me want to scream, debilitating anxiety. I was useless to my family, embarrassed by the downward spiral I had allowed myself to get into, and I prayed for bedtime so that I could escape the prison my mind was during the day. Is this what my life would be like forever? I was a strong woman, and I couldn't get myself out of the house for fear of a massive anxiety attack. I was utterly broken. I had zero confidence, no self-worth, and I was becoming a shell of a human being.

My redemption story started here and has continued since that time. I got some help, I prayed a little more, and my confidence resurfaced. I wasn't healed and I wasn't whole, but I was about to embark on a five-year journey to God redefining who I am and who He has called me to be. The most empowering thing we can do as women is know who we are and not accept the things that people say we are. Our solid foundation in Christ is how we can be world-changers. When we are sure of our identity in Christ, we are able to follow God's direction for our lives without fear of judgment because the world's opinion of us is not the one that matters.

My prayer for you reading this study is that God would speak to your heart in the most intimate, personalized way. I pray that this study opens your eyes to the wonder that is YOU, and that you would hold tightly to these truths each day of your life. You, girlfriend, are a daughter of the King of the Universe, a co-heir with Him, and His Spirit lives in you each and everyday. What can't you do?

———————

Now we look inside, and what we see is that anyone united with the Messiah gets a fresh start, is created new. The old life is gone; a new life burgeons!
2 Corinthians 5:17 MSG

———————

Rate your understanding of who God made you to be on a scale from 1-10.

Now, rate your belief in that truth.

Let's bump that number up near a 9, shall we?

This month, we are going to release and replace. Right now, in your quiet space, speak out loud to the Lord. Release your old self to the Lord, and ask Him to replace it with the real you, the new you, your truest identity.

God, you are my Creator. You took special care in creating my unique personality, characteristics, body type, and spirit. Thank You for seeing me, the real me. I release to You the lies I have believed that I am anything less than what Your Word tells me I am, and I ask you to replace it with the truth. My heart is open and ready to accept what You know to be true about me. I am ready.

You,

GIRLFRIEND, ARE A

daughter

OF THE KING OF THE UNIVERSE,

a co-heir

WITH HIM, AND HIS SPIRIT

lives in you

EACH AND EVERYDAY.

What can't you do?

day two

YOU ARE VERY GOOD

Let's start at the very beginning of the Word. God is busying Himself with the creation of the world. He has land and sea, fish and birds, snakes, for whatever reason, and He stops. Something isn't right. This beauty and splendor is lacking the most important element: mankind. Did the world need us? No. Did God need us? No. If anything, He needed us like He needed a hole in the head.

In Genesis 1:26 God is speaking to the Trinity, and says, "Guys, let's make mankind in Our image, and they will take care of this world." Verse 27 goes on to say that He created man and woman in His own image. Then, He blessed them. Straight out of the gate, we are blessed by the Creator of the world. You are not cursed - you are blessed. James 3:9-10 tells us that what God has blessed man cannot curse. From the moment mankind breathed its first breath, we were blessed. Then, God steps back to observe what He has made, and He calls it very good. He looked at you, girl, and declares that you are very good (verse 31). He made you intimately and personally, and He calls you by name. You are made in His image. You are very good.

So, then, why, when you hear this, do you cringe? Why do you stand in front of the mirror poking at your cellulite or your twin flap (where my twin mamas at?) and curse your body? Why do you believe that you are far from very good, far from the image of God? Why do you do things to your body in secret in attempts to be thinner, bustier, taller, bootylicious? Why are you not content with the perfect creation standing before your mirror? I have some theories.

At any given moment at any point in a day, you have access to millions of photos of people whose lives are plastered all over Facebook and Instagram. The highlight reel of our lives is on display 24/7 thanks to technology. I can search Santorini and find hundreds of beautiful, model-type women, sipping champagne, overlooking the Mediterranean in the most high-fashion swimwear. Then, I can search farmhouse and be inundated with millions of beautifully decorated homes that are clean, white, and organized with only the best pieces. I can search Bible journaling, and be hit with photos of women who are, clearly, reading the Bible more poignantly and at a greater depth because their Instagram photo shows me just how perfectly her "study" set-up is. Her Bible is color-coded, her handwriting is precise, her pens and highlighters are arranged just so, and she has the perfect caption depicting the most ethereal moment she has just had with the Lord. These searches were all done in under two minutes. In two minutes, I have learned that I need to lose weight and make more money to 1. buy new clothes and 2. travel more. I have also learned that my messy house with Cheetos hand-prints on the walls and dirty floors must be hidden from the world lest anyone know that Joanna Gaines was unable to wave her farmhouse wand over my tract home. Plus, I am less of a woman of God because my Bible studying times are short or non-existent, and I can't for the life of me get as much meat off of those bones as these women have gotten because I'm clearly far less intelligent than they are. Two minutes was all it took to reduce myself to nothing. Two minutes was all it took to take my worth and my confidence from a healthy 8 to a solid 2 because social media tells me that I lack things that will, inevitably, make my life happier, more fulfilling, and more interesting to my audience. Where are the Oreos? Because I'm going to eat the entire package while watching Grey's Anatomy and sob into my Diet Coke because #balance.

In two short minutes, I have utterly decimated the woman whose face God took in His hands, stared deep into her eyes, and whispered, "Daughter, you are perfect. You are blessed and you are my handiwork. Hey, guys! Come look at her - she's perfect!"

YOU, precious one, are His handiwork. He handcrafted you to the exact specifications. Do you know why He paid such extreme attention to detail? Because we all fit together. No two of us are alike because we each fulfill a piece of His story that only we can tell. Romans 12 tells us that we are all given gifts and talents, along with our personalities and

13

our characteristics to fulfill a specific role in the church. We work together through the Holy Spirit to fulfill our duty. Verse 18 goes on to say that God arranged His creation, in the body, each one of them, as He chose. Girl, He.chose.you. He chose you to have your grace and charisma, He chose your place in this world, He chose your family, He chose your destiny, and He wants to walk you through each step to live your very best life. Joshua 8:8 tells us that He wants us to listen to His Word so that we prosper and are successful. Because He loves you so much!

My prayer for you reading this study is that God would speak to your heart in the most intimate, personalized way. I pray that this study opens your eyes to the wonder that is YOU, and that you would hold tightly to these truths each day of your life. You, girlfriend, are a daughter of the King of the Universe, a co-heir with Him, and His Spirit lives in you each and everyday. What can't you do?

Then God said, "Let us make mankind in our image, after our likeness. And let them have dominion over the fish of the sea and over the birds of the heavens and over the livestock and over all the earth and over every creeping thing that creeps on the earth."

You,

PRECIOUS ONE, ARE

His handiwork.

day three

YOU ARE RAISED UP

Our lives are so often defined by our struggle, by our hurts, and by our rejections. It's easy to take the sum of our losses and the depths to which they have hurt us and allow the enemy to tell us just how little we matter. We are quick to accept our faults and our weaknesses as our defining characteristics, and even quicker to reject compliments that would give us a more accurate description of our character.

When we are rejected by people, it cuts right to the core. Why? The way that God designed us was for connection and companionship, so when one of those connections is damaged, our sense of belonging is crippled. It can even begin a ripple effect in our other relationships as that rejection is shared with others. And let's be entirely honest: the age we are living in can make those rejections seem so much deeper and more glaring. With our lives plastered all over social media, the FOMO can be deep and cutting. The beauty of rejection is that it is no respecter of persons. No one is immune to being rejected, and in that sentiment, there is a sense of peace. You and I will both experience rejection at some point in our lives, and because of that, we can relate to each other, if in no other way, through rejection. They will look different on both of us, but we will both experience it. How the rejection is internalized, dealt with, and manifested is where we will differ even further. Our unique personalities and past experiences will determine how we cope.

The rejection will penetrate and give us a false sense of identity. A simple snub can cut to the core of who you believe you are if you are not rooted deeply in the Word and what God says about you. The world may be telling you that you are unworthy, but quite the opposite is true in the Word. In Psalm 27:10, David knows deep in his soul that even if his parents were to turn their backs on him, the Lord would always be there. There is no mistake too great or hurt too deep to keep God from standing right next to you.

Rejection hurts. Period. End of story. And it is ok to admit it and take it to Jesus. Get in your car and scream and yell and cry until you have adequately conveyed to God how much the rejection cut you. The cool thing about the God we serve is that He knows the greatest rejection in the history of the world. He hung on a cross while the world rejected Him so that you could live forever with Him. The Son of God is not immune to rejection. So, He gets it. When your heart is broken, He can empathize with you because He, too, was rejected by man. Here's where your mind is going to be blown: the degree to which we let hurt and rejection in is our decision. A woman who is so deeply rooted in the truth of who she is and what her purpose on earth is cannot be uprooted by rejection. Her roots are so deep in the Word of God that her leaves may shift, but she is firmly planted and won't sway. She has accepted God's words over her, and not only that, but has taken action. She walks in confidence because of Who her Creator is. She understands that this life is fleeting, and her eternal life is the real show. She knows that there is zero condemnation in Christ because He has already paid the price for all the gazillion times that she has screwed up. And she knows that grace and mercy cover her life because her God loves her, raised her up, and seated her in heavenly places next to Him. He is proud of her and wants to show her off.

You see, she knows how much the God of the universe adores her and that He sees the truest version of her. He created every square inch of her, and calls her good. So, a little rejection is going to roll off of her because she doesn't need to worry about what others think of her. She is rooted deep, and those roots don't sway.

God, being rich in mercy, because of the great love with which he loved us...and raised us up with him and seated us with him in the heavenly places in Christ Jesus, so that in the coming ages he might show the immeasurable riches of his grace in kindness toward us in Christ Jesus.
Ephesians 2:4,6-7 ESV

How deep are your roots? Do you sway easily?

Release any rejection you have felt over the years. Forgive those people for the words they said or the way they treated you. Ask God to replace it with the truth that you are firmly rooted.

Lord, my heart aches for the words spoken over me, and the times that people hurt me. Give me the words to speak over my own heart when the rejection washes over me. Thank You God that Your Word tells me that I am raised up with You, unmoved by hurt and rejection. Help me to keep my eyes fixed on You.

Her roots
ARE SO DEEP IN THE
Word of God
THAT HER LEAVES MAY SHIFT,
but she is
FIRMLY PLANTED AND
won't sway.

day four

YOU ARE LOVED

Think back on the moments when you first fell in love. I'd like to stop here and say, "I win!" And I'll prove it to you!

You see, I dated my very best friend my senior year of high school. The official 2002 class mantra was "are they dating yet?" Everyone knew it was coming, us included, but it wasn't until just before our senior year that we got it together and started dating.

The following year, living in southern California, we decided to buy each other year-long Disneyland passes for Christmas. For those of you in California, those passes were only $99 then. That is how old we are. We spent a lot of time at Disneyland, riding our favorite rides over and over. Disneyland at Christmastime is especially magical because everything is more magical at Christmas. The characters look especially dapper in their Christmas duds, a massive Christmas tree greets you as you enter the park, and twinkle lights adorn every square inch of the park. Every night, a Christmas parade begins, so in a race to beat the crowds, from the very back of the park, Josh and I ran as fast we could to get to the entrance of the park. When we had reached the Christmas tree, I turned to face him and he kissed me. Right at that moment, snow began to fall all over Main Street.

YOU GUYS! It was straight out of a movie! I still get butterflies when I tell that story! I spent the rest of the time we dated, pleading with the Lord to let me marry this boy. I'd barter each night with God. We got married in 2007, and that's still one of our favorite memories.

I always thought it was a little odd that the description of a bride and groom is the same way we are seen to God. It seemed a little goofy. Until it clicked.

That passion and excitement that I felt in those moments as a teenager are mirrored in the way that your God sees you. That heart-racing, sweaty-palmed moments are how the Lord feels about you. His overwhelming desire is full union with you. He doesn't want to miss a moment with you, so He sent His Son to bridge that gap.

God loved you so much that He sent His Child to die a horrific death in order that we might live forever in heaven. He didn't send Him to wag His finger at us - He sent Him in the name of love. This was His last-ditch effort to save us from an eternity of damnation. He did that for you.

Jesus furthers that statement in John 15 by saying, *just as much as the Father loves you, I love you. Spend time with me in this relationship. Yeah, I'm telling you some things to avoid, but that's because I want you to be full of joy, not walking around plagued by sin and sadness. I'm choosing you. Choose me! Choose this life where we can be together.*

Then, we get to take that example of love and love each other. 1 John 4:7 tells us that we love each other because God has shown us how to love. His selfless example shows us how to love the people in our life without expectation or reciprocation. We get to choose God each and every day because He doesn't force us to love Him back. We get to decide daily to greet Him, invite Him into our day, and then, learn more and more how to love selflessly and wholly.

You are loved. Accept it. The thoughts and feelings that you don't deserve it are lies. Just say yes. His death is over and done with, and now, He just wants you to choose to love him back. Do it. It's a wild ride.

For God so loved the world that he gave his one and only Son, that whoever believes in him shall not perish but have eternal life. For God did not send his Son into the world to condemn the world, but to save the world through him. John 3:16-17 NIV

Do you choose God? Do you choose the road less traveled? Do you believe He loved you so much that He died for you?

Release the lies that you are unlovable and unwanted. Replace them with the most incredible verse in the entire Bible: He gave His Son up for *you*.

Jesus, it is unimaginable that You would die for me. That kind of love makes my head spin. Lord, help me to grasp this deep love You have for me. Forgive me for the times that I have believed that I am not worthy of Your love. I accept Your love and Your sacrifice. Help me to no longer take it for granted.

You

ARE LOVED.

Accept it.

day five

YOU ARE NOT HER

Take a moment to think about the women in your life you admire. What draws you to them? What is it about them that makes you stop and pay attention? There's no wrong answer because each of us is drawn to different people for different reasons.

We each have a "her." She is the one who we admire, possibly covet, and even copy to an extent. Her highlight reel is everything we desire for ourselves. Her kids are put together, her husband adores her, her hair is always perfectly tressed, her style is fabulous, her talents are flawless. If we could just be more like HER, we'd be

_____.

We change our hairstyles, we buy the same clothes, we start speaking like her, and we model our lives after her because something about her life makes us feel like she has it together. And if we can imitate her, then we, too, will

26

have it all together. Let me unpack all of those ridiculous untruths for you now.

First of all, we are not supposed to have it all together, and I defy you to find one person who actually does. God created us for community with Him and with each other for a reason: it's not good that we should be alone. You have the family and friends that you have because you are created for it. 1 Corinthians 2:12 tells us that He gave us the Holy Spirit Who knows our thoughts as well as God's. He acts as a go-between for us to understand our Father even better. You have a Counselor on retainer 24/7. So, when you start believing Satan when he tells you that "she" has her poop in a group, wag your finger at him and tell him to get behind you. Not today, Satan.

Secondly, 1 Corinthians 12 tells us that we all have a purpose. If you look at the human body, you can't have all arms. It doesn't work. You need a head, legs, a torso, and maybe even some junk in the trunk. The body of Christ is no different. Her talents are her talents because they tell one piece of the story. The gifts that God gave you are so that you are equipped to tell your story. When you wrestle with your gifts and what your section of the story is you are negating the incredible purpose that God has placed on your life. You are not less than her. She is not less than you. You both have value, and you both add value to others.

All it takes is a whisper from the devil to get us off track. A simple snide comment from him is how our culture has become so nasty with each other. We let him whisper in our ear without shutting him down, and suddenly, we have a deep hatred for this woman. Jealousy is now coursing through our veins, and what was created to be this beautiful, cohesive body working together, has turned into a disjointed, dysfunctional mess. If your hand is fighting your foot, you aren't going to get very far. This is exactly the picture that Paul paints for us. If one of us suffers, the whole body suffers. So, if we are actively dealing with jealousy, we are causing the whole machine to suffer. Ouch!

Here's the thing: she can't do what you can do. Your purpose is not her purpose. Her story is not your story, and her story does not take away from your story. Our stories are interwoven for a greater purpose. And if we all copied each other, our purpose wouldn't be fulfilled, we wouldn't impact the people we are supposed to impact, and our lives won't tell the story that God planned for us. Your stories are equally important - they both need to be told.

Her story does not negate your story.

Tell your own story, fulfill your own purpose, and walk free knowing that there is no one like you and only you can be the best you.

God arranged the members in the body, each one of them as He chose.
1 Corinthians 12:18 ESV

Who is your "her?" Release her to the Lord, bless her for who she is, and replace the lie that you need to be more like her with the truth that who you are is integral to telling your own story.

What story is God asking you to tell? Where has He placed you to fulfill your purpose?

I find that so many women are unsure of what their calling is or where they fit in. This one isn't always clear, but I promise you that God will show you your purpose if you ask.

Father, thank You for giving me a key role in this world. Thank You for my talents and gifts that only I can use. Thank You that my story is just as important as "hers." God, I need direction. Show me what You want me to do. Show me Your plan for my life, and then, bring it to completion.

Her story

DOES NOT

negate

YOUR STORY.

day six

YOU HAVE A BRIGHT FUTURE

I have control issues. I like predictability. I hate surprises. If at all possible, I enlist the help of my girlfriends to tell my husband what to get me for birthdays and holidays. If he has already purchased something, I am not above snooping. I've even opened a Christmas present a time or two when I'm home alone, and then, wrapped it back up as though nothing has happened. Sorry, honey.

I just don't like surprises. I like the comfort of knowing, good or bad, what is coming down the pike so I can hunker down. I attribute this to three things: my being the typical, type-A, firstborn, my 15-year struggle with anxiety disorder, and my being a human. I'm going to throw in some trust issues as well.

My earliest memory is when I was just shy of 4 years old.

31

You see, my Uncle Ron was stalked and killed by his ex-girlfriend. I remember exactly where I was in our living room when the phone rang. It was late, and I was supposed to be in bed. I knew something was wrong, but I don't know how much I retained that night. The next thing I remember was the entire family meeting at my grandparents house and spending the night.

Whether I knew it consciously or not, that night opened a door to my little spirit. Fear. We all knew intense, real fear in that moment. I would go on to have years of insomnia because I was just terrified to close my eyes at night. The fear of the dark, the fear of the future, the fear of the unknown were all plaguing me. How could I trust a God Who allowed something so horrific to happen? How could I possibly not fear my future when it didn't feel secure? How could I believe that He is faithful to finish what He started in me?

By 17, I was having massive anxiety attacks. Doctors would try to reason the anxiety out of me, but what it came down to was complete and utter fear of the unknown. I craved control and predictability. As you can imagine, I began to control my food. First, I ate like I was starving. My daily calorie intake was scary. When that got too wild, I swung the opposite way and starved myself. For a good portion of time, I drank only caffeine and ate one Lean Cuisine a day. I needed to be in control.

I lost all semblance of control when I found out I was pregnant with the twins. I was on bedrest at 13 weeks, in labor at 27 weeks, and on mandatory hospital bed rest for 6 weeks. It was the most out of control I had ever been in my life. It was that experience where God began showing me what He meant in Jeremiah 29. You see, I thought I needed to know the plans, but why? His promise was that He would fulfill His plans for my life, and that they were good.

If you've been in the Christian realm at all, you'll likely have heard the verse Jeremiah 29:11: "For I know the plans I have for you - plans to prosper you and not to harm you, plans to give you hope and a future." Do you remember the trust game from when you were a kid? You'd get in front of a friend, they'd promise to catch you, and you'd fall back? If they were good friends, they'd catch you. If they were hilarious friends, they'd step to the side and let you fall! That's what I see when I hear this verse. This is the ultimate trust game. Do you trust God to do what's best for you? Do you trust Him to lead you? Do you trust that He sees a bigger picture? Do you trust that when your heart breaks that it is all going to work out?

In Jeremiah 29:10-14, Jeremiah is speaking to the exiles and telling them, "listen, He knows what you need. He knows the end of the story, and guess what? You win!" Jeremiah never once says that it's all going to be a cakewalk, but that God will bring it all full circle. This life is going to be a train wreck. Sure, there will be good moments, great seasons, and amazing people, but our victory is not on this side. We win when this place goes up in smoke. He's going to walk through this life with us, speak to us, listen to us, and fulfill our purpose, but it's not up to us what that looks

33

like. His plans are good. He's in control. Did we actually believe we were ever in control?

_____

I know the plans that I laid out for you, and oooh, girl. They are really good. Your future is bright.
Jeremiah 29:11

_____

Do you trust God's plans for your life?

Do you believe He will fulfill it?

Release the lies that you are in control and that God wants to do anything less than show you the incredible future He laid out for you. Replace these lies with the knowledge that He made plans that are for your good.

Lord, I lay down my control issues at Your feet. I know You chuckle when You watch me try to take control of my life. You see the bigger picture and I don't. Help me to lean into that truth so that I can take a deep breath and let You lead. Thank You for thinking of me, for planning a bright future for my good. Thank You that You will bring my story to fulfillment for the benefit of everyone. Thank You for being such an incredible storyteller.

God

WILL BRING IT ALL

full circle.

day seven

YOU ARE CALLED

I hated P.E. as a kid. I was a girl, I threw like a girl, and I ran like a girl. Occasionally, the boys and girls classes would combine, and we'd play a game together. Guess who was picked last a lot of the time? I went through a season where I could whack a ball into the outfield, but it was short-lived. The biggest thing about being picked last was the utter embarrassment that I wasn't cool. As I got older, I found that saying I had cramps would get me out of this fun popularity contest, and I fully plan on passing that information on to my daughter when the time comes.

I went to a small school where we weren't very good at many sports, but our high school boys' basketball team was incredible. The gym was packed full of both school's fans, and we had pretty good rivalries with other Christian schools. No, it was not all wholesome, Christian fun.

Unfortunately, this talent did not transfer to the girls'

basketball team. We had one good player. In the 10th grade, I got a wild hair to try out for the team. I knew the basics about basketball because I dated a basketball player for about two seconds, our team was amazing, I was at every game, and I was a Lakers' fan. I wasn't one of those girls who cheered for them to score a touchdown at a basketball game. I was, however, a complete and total dork on the court myself.

In my first ever game, someone dared to pass me the ball and I ran the wrong way down the court to the other teams' basket. Even as I write this, my hands and feet are sweaty, and the embarrassment is real. Thankfully, the stands were almost completely empty. I quit the team the following week, and never looked back. I wasn't good at playing basketball, but I could watch them like a champ.

I was annoyed that God hadn't me a better athlete and that I didn't have the inclination to want to play sports. Instead, He gave me the nerdy talents: school secretary and yearbook editor. What I didn't see then is entirely clear to me now.

You see, He picked me to do some really cool things. I wouldn't be clacking on this keyboard if He hadn't given me this affinity for writing and women's ministry. In Romans 8:28-30, He tells us that there is a greater purpose that we are working towards. He gave each of us gifts and talents that all work together for our good. Before He even created me, He had a plan for my life. Me. Some girl in the middle of the United States. He called me. He called me to be a leader. He called me to a greater purpose than being good at basketball. And not only that, He justified me. How do I know that? His Word tells me.

He thought of you. When He was deciding who you would be, He made decisions. He intricately decided on your hair color, your face shape, your gifts, your talents, your shoe size, your personality, and your purpose. The Creator of the universe stopped and thought of you. Girl, He handcrafted you and made you exactly how you are, and it is very good (Genesis 1:31).

You were chosen, called, justified, and then, glorified. Straighten your tiara, princess. You are one special creation.

And we know that in all things God works for the good of those who love him, who have been called according to his purpose. For those God foreknew he also predestined to be conformed to the image of his Son, that he might be the first-born among many brothers and sisters. And those he predestined, he also called; those he called, he also justified; those he justified, he also glorified.
Romans 8:28-30 NIV

List 10 gifts and talents God has given you. No, I mean it!
Write them down!

God gave you those gifts to do what you need to do in this life.

Release the lies that you have no gifts or talents. Release the belief that you aren't called to greatness. Now, replace those with the truth of Romans 8.

Your Word tells me that I am chosen, called, justified and glorified. Lord, most days, I feel like a train hit me and that I don't measure up. But you know what? My feelings don't matter. Your Word tells me that You picked me, called me, justified me, and glorified me. I don't feel it, but I accept it and I choose to believe it because it's what Your Word says. Let these truths sink into my heart, so that one day, I wake up believing them.

You

WERE CHOSEN

called,

AND JUSTIFIED.

straighten your

TIARA

princess.

day eight

YOU ARE SEEN

Why do you Instagram? No, really. Take a step back and really think about what makes you want to use Instagram. I'll wait.

What did you decide? What's the real reason? If your answer isn't "to be seen," then you can skip this chapter. If, however, you are like the rest of us, your driving force is being seen, but why? Why do we so desperately want the world to see how perfectly plated our lunch is or how this one corner of the house is actually clean?

I'm picking on Instagram because it's entirely picture -driven, and I am writing this as much to you as to myself. I have a color palette, a specific edit that changes only slightly, a certain way I caption my images, a time of day I post, and a specific feeling I like to evoke in my images. Instagram can be a form of art if you take the time to pay close attention to detail. Some of my very favorite

Instagrammers create such an ethereal experience in their squares that I can get lost for hours, wishing that my house was clean or that my hair wasn't greasy.

As our culture has moved and evolved and changed, our desire to be seen and to stand out has grown. Because our entire lives are now showcased on some or all social media platforms, we have created a facade that we hide behind. This is not necessarily all bad. That facade protects us from backlash, as well as a way to show the best versions of ourselves while being just open and honest enough to be relatable. This is a level of vulnerability that we deem acceptable for the masses.

I don't know about you, but my desire to be seen is reflected in my credit card statement. You can see when I am struggling the most to look or act a certain way. When I am at my pettiest, the amount of likes on a photo can make or break my day. When I am at my least confident, the number of followers can really destroy my self-worth. But when I take a step back and think about the greater picture and the point of my life, I can harrumph because the Creator of everything sees *me*, bends His ear to *me*, talks to *me*.

It's so easy to look around this world and feel so small. It's easy to feel like you are lost in a sea of girls who want to be seen and heard. It's easy to feel like you need to make your mark on this world by finding your unique voice, but God tells us repeatedly that He is watching us, talking to us, walking with us, growing us, loving us.

43

He sees you. Nothing else matters.

Jesus turned and saw her. "Take heart, daughter," he said, "your faith has healed you." And the woman was healed at that moment.
Matthew 9:22 NIV

Do you feel compelled to share only the very best about your life?

Are you scared to show the world the real you?

Release your need to be validated and seen by the world, and replace that emptiness with the truth: your Creator sees you, bends His ear to hear you, and talks to you.

God, I want to be seen. Thank You for seeing me, the real me, and loving me enough to send Your Son to die for me. I lay down my need to be seen by the world, and ask You to show me that only Your attention matters. Thank You for bending Your ear to me when I talk to You. Thank You for making me feel so important.

He

SEES YOU.

Nothing else

MATTERS.

day nine

YOU ARE VALUABLE

I have three gorgeous kids. Like, truly attractive children. I not-so-secretly worried before I had kids that only the bad parts of our features would come together, and we'd have to cross our fingers for really incredible personalities. We were blessed: they are beautiful AND have great personalities.

At 24-years-old, my biological clock had taken complete control of my brain and turned me into a crazy person. I woke up one day and was ready to have a baby. My husband of two years suggested a dog. After we got our puppy, the itch for kids hadn't been scratched, and on my 25th birthday, my incredibly thoughtful husband bought me a card and wrote a letter to me telling me all of the reasons that I would be an amazing mother, ending with the question, "are you ready?" I know - he's amazing!

We started trying immediately to have a baby, and two

weeks later, I saw two faint pink lines. We were going to have a December baby, and I was over the moon. Our due date was December 8, 2009 and I told everyone I knew. What I didn't know is that this was the beginning of a really hard season.

I also didn't know that 1 in 4 women have miscarriages. Not only did I not know that, but I didn't know that I would be someone who would go on to have five miscarriages. I couldn't understand how this could be my story. Teenagers were getting pregnant in the back of cars, and I couldn't keep a pregnancy for longer than 7 weeks. How could this be the best plan for my life? I must have really made God angry for Him to make me suffer like this. What a cruel joke to play on me by giving me this overwhelming desire to be a mother only to rip it away from me.

I went on to have another miscarriage in June of that year, and against my wishes, we took a break. We were cleared by my doctor to try again in December, and I sobbed in my bathroom on December 7th. The next day was my original due date, and here I was, empty womb. A failure. I was failing at being a woman. My body was made to create babies and I had failed.

The following morning, I woke up to intense nausea. I was also late. My husband finally told me to take a test. I knew I wasn't pregnant, but I did it anyway. This time, the two darkest lines I'd ever seen appeared. On my original due date, I found out I was pregnant, and it was as though God was smiling on me, saying, "I told you I'd take care of you."

In August 2010, we had our first baby, a daughter, and she was perfect. The "curse" had been broken. My body just needed to get those two miscarriages out of the way, and now, we could have as many babies as we wanted.

I went on to have three more miscarriages. I remember pleading with God that I would do whatever He wanted if He would just let me carry these babies to term. I'd go to church more, I'd tithe more, I'd stop swearing - anything if He would just let me have these babies that I so desperately wanted to have. My faith was non-existent. In that season, I felt like He was proving Himself to be the vengeful, angry, Old Testament God who didn't love me or care for me. I had, clearly, done something wrong, and He was making me pay for it.

After my 5th miscarriage, I was poked and prodded on a weekly basis. My doctor intervened with fertility medicine, and in September 2013, the two pink lines showed up once again. I scheduled an appointment for an ultrasound, and nearly fell off the table when the technician announced that I was pregnant with twins. God has the most annoying sense of humor sometimes! I went on to have the rockiest twin pregnancy in history, but in May of 2014, I gave birth to perfect baby boys, who are now 4-years-old.

God had seen me through the darkest time in my adult life. I questioned His faithfulness, His love for me, and my own worth. In Matthew 6:25-26, He tells us that such care and tenderness goes into feeding the ravens, and why wouldn't He take even greater care of the people that He created and sent His Son to die for? He wasn't angry at me - He was preparing me for a literal double portion and for a life of ministry to women.

I went on to meet tons of women who'd shared a similar experience, and I was able to love them, minister to them, and encourage them because of what I'd gone through, and isn't that the point, girls? We're here to help each other, bless each other, pray for each other, and hold up each other's arms when we can no longer hold them up ourselves.

———————

"Therefore I tell you, do not worry about your life, what you will eat or drink; or about your body, what you will wear. Is not life more than food, and the body more than clothes? Look at the birds of the air; they do not sow or reap or store away in barns, and yet your heavenly Father feeds them. Are you not much more valuable than they? Can any one of you by worrying add a single hour to your life?
Matthew 6:25-27 NIV

Have you ever gone through a season where it felt like God was working against you?

Are you in that season now? Or are you on the other side of it? Do you see clearly now that you are past it?

Release the lies that you aren't valuable and that God can't use your story to minister to others. Replace these with the truth that God takes great care of you, and will see you through to the other side of this battle.

———————

I know that You work all things together for my good, and I accept that. Lord, I don't know that I can see how this situation will benefit me or others, but I ask You to bring these to fulfillment. Use me to help others. Use my battles to bless others. Give me a way to use my story to minister to people going through the same things. Use me, God. Use my story.

We're here to

HELP EACH OTHER,

bless each other,

PRAY FOR EACH OTHER,

and hold each other's

ARMS UP.

day ten

YOU ARE FREE

Have you ever royally screwed up? Not a small, minute biff, but a life-altering, I-can't-ever-take that-back kind of mess? I'm sure it's just me, but for giggles, let's pretend that you have done at least one thing in your life that was a massive blunder.

As I sit here with the cursor blinking at me, my laundry list of mistakes is beginning to flood my mind. There are times that I shared a small secret, and then, ones that shame me even now. I can't even give you the one horrific event in my life because they all seem to measure to the same level of disaster. I'm sure you can't relate to this at all because you have your life in much better order than I do.

There was a very dark period in my life where I didn't even want to exist any longer. I had ruined so many relationships that I pulled away from any remaining friends that I had, believing that I was going to ruin them. I believed every single thing that was said about me by other people and the things that I had called myself. What was the point of being here if this was how I was going to feel? Where was the grace that covered a multitude of sins? I certainly didn't feel it or see it.

I knew the verses, I knew the Christian mantras. I could quote grace without batting an eyelash, but I never once believed that I was worthy of that grace. Grace was for everyone else and every other circumstance. It wasn't until I heard a message about grace a couple of years ago that it finally clicked for me. By saying that grace wasn't for me, I was saying that Jesus' sacrifice wasn't enough. (I can feel the collective groan!)

The Creator of the universe sent His perfect, flawless Son to the earth to bridge the gap between man & Father, and I was telling Him that it wasn't enough and that I couldn't accept grace because it only stretched so far. The worst part about this was the many women who believed just as I did. And even worse was hearing that they didn't believe the words in Scripture calling us His chosen & precious ones (James 1 something), children of God (John 1:12), saved and called (2 Timothy 1:9), anointed, forgiven, blessed, holy, loved (Ephesians 1). The world had broken them down, chewed them up, and spit them out. Their spirits were crushed, and too many ugly things were now on repeat in their own minds for any of these truths to penetrate to their heart.

I would venture to guess that if you are a woman reading this that more than one person has said something, whether true or untrue, to you that was cruel, hurtful, and mean. That some kind of curse was spoken over your life, and as a result, that girl inside of you, who knows that she was created by God, cowered a little deeper and a little longer each time those words were said. And I would guess that there are words ping-ponging in your head right now that cut you so deeply it's as if it's happening right this second.

Precious girl, lift up your head. Your Creator is so much bigger than words. Your Savior loves you so much more deeply than you could ever actually understand. Your Comforter is grieved by your hurt. Your Redeemer has washed away your mistakes from His record. You are set free. You are not what you've done. You are not what people have said about you as a result of your mistakes. Your sins are removed as far as the east is from the west.

Your sin does not define you.

If you believe the Word of God, then you can cling to that truth and hold onto it for dear life. Romans 6:7 tells us we are not defined by our sins because we are released from them forever. And why is that? Because God so loved the world that He gave His one and only Son, that whoever believes in Him shall not perish but have eternal life. He died for every lie, every dishonor, every swear word, every hateful thought, every time we wanted to hide a body, every ugly, nasty thought we could ever have, and His death was enough for you.

If that ain't love, I don't know what is.

...anyone who has died has been set free from sin.
Romans 6:7 NIV

————————

Have you forgiven yourself for your mistakes and sins? God has, so it's time that you did the same.

Release the words, the lies, the curses, and the sins. They do not define you. Replace those with the truth that your sins are removed as far as the east is from the west.

————————

I don't deserve it, but I accept Your gift of freedom from my sin. Forgive me for the times I have let my sin become my identity. Thank You for paying the biggest price for my life. Thank You for removing my stains, and making me whole again. Thank You for being such a forgiving God. Thank You for loving me.

Your sin

DOES NOT

define you.

day eleven

YOU ARE CHOSEN

My daughter is 7-years-old, and we are in the funniest phase with her. She wants to know where the heck God came from. He created us, but who created Him? If you stop and try to understand it, you will likely get a headache. In our finiteness, it is utterly impossible to understand a God that just exists outside of space and time. As a grown woman, I struggle to grasp it, so teaching a 7-year-old is buckets of fun.

Her next question is always, "why did God even make us?" Ephesians 1:4 tells us that before the foundation of the world, He loved us. We are made in the image of God (Genesis 1:26), He is part of a trinity, and we are all made for community (Genesis 2:18). These three things give us a little insight into God the Creator. You are here because He wanted you here. You are here because, without you, the world wasn't exactly right. You are here because, before light and darkness were created, you were loved by God.

God's love for you doesn't stop there. Ephesians 1 goes on to tell us that because He loved you, He chose to make you holy and without fault. Did you read day 10?! Go back and read it again. Your sins don't make you the person you are. Your Creator has chosen to make you without blame. And then! I'm not even done! And then, He chose you for adoption.

I have a younger sister, and like the typical older sister, I let her know that she was adopted. If this lie ever sank in, I really don't know. Just a few years ago, this topic came up in front of our Dad, and I was pretty sure I was about to get thrown over his knee. He couldn't believe that I would say something to my sweet, innocent, little sister like this. Keep in mind, he is the youngest of three boys, so his perspective is skewed. Firstborn siblings, you feel me? She, clearly, wasn't adopted, and all is well, but the best comeback to that lie I have ever heard was, "we picked your sister - we just got stuck with you."

Ephesians 1:5 goes on to tell us that we were adopted. We were orphans, alone in the world, cut off from a God we couldn't understand, but He sent His Son to find us and complete the adoption process. He chose you because He loves you. Plain and simple. There is nothing that will change it, and nothing that can take away from it. The Word says it, and the Word is true.

There's this beautiful quote that pops up on Facebook occasionally that paints such a beautiful picture of the Creator: "How cool is it that the same God Who created mountains and oceans and galaxies looked at you and thought the world needed one of you too."

Precious one, this world wouldn't be complete without you.

For he chose us in him before the creation of the world to be holy and blameless in his sight. In love he predestined us for adoption to sonship through Jesus Christ, in accordance with his pleasure and will.
Ephesians 1:4-5 NIV

Do you truly believe that you are chosen by God? Do you believe that He picked you?

Release the lie that you are the red-headed stepchild no one really wanted, and replace it with the truth that you were chosen before the world was even created.

God, thank You for choosing me. Thank You for loving me that much. Thank You for making me holy and blameless. Thank You for the most amazing adoption story ever.

Precious one,

THIS WORLD

wouldn't be

COMPLETE

without you.

day twelve

YOU ARE A CHILD

What's your earliest memory as a kid? Is it Christmas morning one year? Maybe the year you got that first bicycle. I remember that one really well. Iridescent purple frame, white and purple tires, and best of all, a rainbow banana seat. I was over the moon to walk into the living room to see the shiniest, most beautiful bicycle. This was all I had dreamed of for all of my 6 years.

Growing up in southern California meant that we could take the bike for a spin immediately because there is only one season all year long. I suffered through the rest of the family opening their gifts, but once they were all opened, Dad and I headed outside. This was my first "big girl" bike, so it was sans training wheels. I wasn't worried though - as I mentioned before, I was a ~~confident~~ cocky kid. So, I hopped up on my banana seat and immediately fell over and onto the asphalt.

After a few false starts, I was upright and Dad held onto the back of my seat. I began pedaling, he quietly let go, and I fell off. We repeated the pattern until I had gained enough confidence to not panic when he let go. This was the ultimate feeling of freedom for a 6-year-old. I was giddy and free. I trusted that my Dad wouldn't let me break any bones as I learned to ride, and once I had mastered being less of a spaz, I felt the weight of the world lift off of my shoulders. I was now confident that I could do this by myself, but if I needed anything, I could get help from my Dad.

Growing up, I didn't think of God as my Father. In my head, He looked like Charlton Heston-does-Moses, complete with a white beard, white robes, and a scowl firmly set on His face. He wasn't kind, He wasn't fun, He wasn't interested in what I wanted. He was judgmental, grumpy, and generally displeased with me. It wasn't until I became a parent myself that I began to understand God the Father a little better.

Being a mom is hard and I would never lie to you and tell you differently. You go from worrying they aren't breathing as infants to worrying that they are eating too much or not enough to yelling at them to "just settle down for 5 seconds." In every single instance as a parent though, the underlying truth is that you would do anything to help your child. Standing and watching their sweet faces is one of my favorite pastimes. I stand in awe that I created such a beautiful kid who is funny and smart and weird and unique and precious. And I'm a flawed human.

Your Father in heaven is perfect in every way. His heart

breaks when the wicked perish, but is giddy when they stop sinning and turn back to Him (Ezekiel 33:11). He corrects us when we mess up so that we don't get hurt (Proverbs 23:13). He loves us so much that He sent Jesus to patch up our disconnection from Him (John 3:16). And He saves us from an eternity separated from our Papa (Romans 10:9).

Girl, He is holding onto the back of that bicycle as you learn to pedal. He wants you to take a deep breath and relax in His presence. He guides you, walks next to you, looks both ways before you cross, and sits on your bed at night before you fall asleep just as your earthly father would. You are His child. You are the apple of His eye. You are the reason He created all of this. And your name is engraved in the palm of His hand like a tattoo (Isaiah 49:16).

———————

You are all sons of God through faith in Christ Jesus.
Galatians 3:26 BSB

———————

Do you trust that your Father has your back? Do you believe that you are His precious daughter He wants to protect?

Release the lie that He is a mean, old dad, waiting to rebuke you. Replace that with the love He has for you as His child. Accept that He is completely enamored with you.

Father God, thank You for being a good, good Father. Thank You for choosing me as your child. Thank You for caring for me as a parent. Forgive me for the times that I have acted out of turn, but thank You for being slow to anger with me.

Your name
IS ENGRAVED
in the palm of
HIS HAND
like a tattoo.

day thirteen

YOU ARE COMFORTED

I have this unbelievably cozy blanket that was given to me as a housewarming gift. It is exactly the right size to curl up on the couch, and make sure all my arms and legs are covered. I love to snuggle up in this blanket, turn on our fake fireplace, and watch the TV after the kids have all gone to sleep.

There are two reasons I love this blanket so much: it's the most comfortable thing I could possibly wrap myself in and it was given to me by someone I love. There is something in its fibers that is comforting and familiar because this person took the time to pick the perfect blanket out. It fits me perfectly, and hits all of the love languages.

It wasn't until recently that I began to understand the unique-ness of the Trinity and all of the characteristics that come into play for each Member. God was the One in charge, Jesus was the Son, and the Holy Spirit just hung around.

It's a dumbed down explanation, but as I read further and further, I saw how much of a role the Holy Spirit plays.

In John 14, Jesus is still on earth, speaking to His disciples. They are freaking out about His impending death. Peter even tells Him to knock it off. They can't imagine that anything terrible could happen to Christ, and certainly couldn't imagine that if there was a plot against Jesus that He couldn't do something to stop it. He tells them that He has to go get our rooms ready in Heaven, but God the Father is sending a Helper to stay with us. Jesus tells His disciples that He isn't abandoning them, but He was sending His Spirit to stay with us.

I love the way the Amplified Bible unpacks the word Helper: Comforter, Counselor, Intercessor. The Holy Spirit is the cozy, chunky blanket that envelops you. He is the Comforter that you can sink into and divulge your deepest, darkest secrets to. He counsels you as you share with Him your daily struggles. And He prays for you. He intercedes on your behalf to the Father. He's the One Who curls up on the couch with you for a fireside chat.

One of the biggest lies we believe in this day and age is that we are alone. The enemy will try and make you believe that no one feels what you're feeling, and that no one cares about you. 1 Corinthians debunks that lie by telling you that the Spirit of God lives inside of you. You are never alone or uncared for. The next time you feel alone, head to your closet or your bed and find your snuggliest blanket. Wrap yourself up and get quiet before the Lord. Invite Him to wrap His arms around you as you sink into Him, falling deeper into the Comforter.

You are never ever alone, dear girl. He is always just a whisper away.

But the Helper (Comforter, Advocate, Intercessor—Counselor, Strengthener, Standby), the Holy Spirit, whom the Father will send in My name [in My place, to represent Me and act on My behalf], He will teach you all things. And He will help you remember everything that I have told you.
1 John 14:26 AMP

Do you ever feel alone, misunderstood, or abandoned?

Do you believe the lie that no one could understand what you're going through?

Holy Spirit, thank You for being with me always. Thank You for being my Helper in every situation. Thank You for never leaving me. I ask that You would make Your presence known to me right now. Wrap Your arms around me. I want to feel You in this space.

You

ARE NEVER

alone,

DEAR GIRL.

day fourteen

YOU ARE SAVED

I grew up going to Awana each week for most of my elementary career. My Mom was a leader, so she dragged my sister and I there each week. Yes, dragged. Each week we were challenged to study and memorize a Scripture, and each week, I wouldn't bother to learn it until we were in the car heading to Awana. I was a good memorizer - I was not a committer to memory.

In addition to the Scripture challenge each week, there was an altar call at the end of every service. At the ripe old age of 7, I was ready. The altar called was made, I raised my hand, I prayed the prayer, and I got a packet from one of my leaders. When my Mom came to pick me up from class, the leader was elated that I had accepted the Lord into my heart! My Mom replied, "Again?" Apparently, I had prayed the sinner's prayer with her around the age of 4.

For the next few weeks, a leader would get up in front of us and make an altar call to salvation. Each week, I raised my hand, asking for forgiveness and for Jesus to come into my heart. It became a running joke between my parents because Mom would come home and say, "Andrea accepted Jesus into her heart again."

While I was clearly adorable and hilarious, I was slightly confused. I was so terrified of this place called hell, and I knew for sure that I didn't want to go there. I figured that if I got "saved" each week, I was clear, and could go about my days without really worrying. What I missed was that Jesus died once and for all. I missed the point of the Scriptures I was memorizing just so I could get a sticker.

It took me well into my 30's to understand that the Bible is the ultimate truth. Nothing that I hear outside of the Word trumps it. I can believe that I need to say the sinner's pray multiple times to ensure my spot in heaven, but what finally clicked not too long ago was that, if the Word says it, it's my job to accept it. No matter what you believe, no matter what has been said about you, no matter what you have seen in the news, the Word of God is the truth of who you are and who God sees you as.

I look back at that little blonde-haired, toothless girl and I want to grab her face and read 2 Timothy 1:9 to her. Paul is writing a letter to Timothy, whom he absolutely adores. He tells Timothy, "God saved you and called you to a holy calling, not because of anything you have done because of His grace and His purpose for your life." That's it. End of story. The day you accepted Christ into your heart, you were saved. You have a one-way ticket to the Disneyland of the universe. And not only that but you have purpose.

Do not roll your eyes at me, missy! Verse 9 tells you that you are called to do something amazing with your life. I can't tell you what that is, but you know what? Stop right now and ask God to show you what He wants you to do with your life. Ask Him to replace the lie that you don't have anything to give or offer or that you aren't talented or creative enough. It's just not true. 1 Corinthians 12:18 tells us that God arranged us just so with different gifts, talents, personalities, ways of hearing His voice, ways of reaching the people in our lives.

Spend some time figuring out what those gifts and talents are. Ask the Lord, ask your family, ask your friends. Dig deep and find the unique giftings that God has given you for your life. They won't look like mine, they won't look like your spouse's, they won't look like your friends'. They will be personal, intricate, and special just as God made you. He's really into the personal touch on each of our lives.

God, who saved us and called us to a holy calling, not because of our works but because of His own purpose and grace, which He gave us in Christ Jesus before the ages began.
2 Timothy 1:9 ESV

Because He saved you, He now has a holy calling for you. Do you know what your calling is? Have you taken the time to hone in on it?

Release the lie that you don't have a purpose, and replace it with the truth that you were saved so that you could go out and change the world.

Thank You for saving me from a life apart from You. Thank You that Your grace was big enough to cover my sins. God, I ask that You would show me my holy calling. Open and close doors that will get me there. Let me be a vessel for Your purpose.

You

ARE CALLED

to do something

AMAZING

with your life.

day fifteen

YOU ARE A TEMPLE

At 17, I was the least athletic person you could ever meet. I hated running, I hated sports, I wasn't a cheerleader. I had boobs, a butt, and thighs. I wasn't overweight, but I also wasn't healthy. Attending high school in southern California wasn't too great for the self-confidence, however. Some of the girls that I had grown up with had remained the same size from elementary school through high school. It was incredibly annoying.

I didn't ever develop a good relationship with food. At 10 years old, I had the metabolism of a basketball player and could pound 2 Big Mac's without batting an eyelash. My Grandma warned me that one day I would no longer be able to eat this way, but I rolled my eyes because she, clearly, had no idea what she was talking about.

A short time later, Grandma's warning began to show up in a softer stomach and thicker thighs. Gone were my ab muscles and my stick legs. Those french fries had finally caught up to me. I noticed the differences between my body and the other girls in school, but not enough to let it keep me up at night. It wasn't until 17 that something shifted inside of me. I was stress eating because I was the yearbook editor as well as the student body secretary. I put on 15 pounds my senior year just because I would grab fast food and shove it down my throat when I had time.

I remember when Oprah started counting calories and lost a bunch of weight. I figured I could do the same thing. So, one day, I decided on a 1000-calorie diet. I would drink a SlimFast in the morning, half a sandwich with a small bowl of soup for lunch, and something equally meager in the evening. I started running a few miles a day, and within 6 weeks, I lost 15 pounds. I could suffer through this if it meant that I could drop a couple of pants sizes.

What I failed to understand was the value of proper nutrition, what is required for healthy brain function, as well as the fuel my body needed to get me through the day, plus my new running regimen. When I started to have anxiety attacks, headaches, and tingling in my extremities, I realized that I probably needed to add some more back into my diet.

What I couldn't have known then was that the body that I beat up would go on to have one typical pregnancy and birth, as well as support a twin pregnancy. I also failed to understand that the body that I was hating and hurting was the body that the Holy Spirit was living inside. I had no idea the power that I had living inside of me. I was too busy being ashamed and frustrated with my curves that I didn't see the beauty and intricacy with which my Creator had created me. My body wasn't made to wear a 00 - my body was made to keep twin boys safe for 7 months. See, God knew that my body had to be made differently because my boys would need it. I could never have guessed at 17-years-old that one day I would see the stretch marks and the c-section "shelf," and that I would be proud of the body that I was given.

Romans 8:11 makes me teary when I really stop and unpack the words: the Spirit who raised Jesus from the dead lives inside of me. Me. In my body. He raised the Son of God from the dead, and He is with me in every inhale and exhale, every tear, every contraction, every laugh, every prayer, every moment. He is there, giving me strength, keeping me going.

Your body is incredible. The good, the bad, and the ugly. The Holy Spirit dwells inside of that perfect, complete body, and He is getting you through the best times and the hardest times. Take care of that vessel - He only gave you the one.

And if the Spirit of Him who raised Jesus from the dead is living in you, He who raised Christ from the dead will also give life to your mortal bodies because of His Spirit who lives in you.
Romans 8:11 NIV

Being completely honest with yourself, do you think about the Holy Spirit living inside of your body? Do you treat it as such? Are there things you will change now that you have really taken the time to think about it?

Release the lie that the body you were given is anything less than the image of God, and replace it with the truth that you are a temple for the Holy Spirit. You are a powerhouse!

Lord, forgive me for treating the body You gave me as anything less than amazing. Thank You for designing me so perfectly and intricately. I need Your help accepting and believing that my body is perfect. Lord, I release the standards that I have placed on myself, and ask You to replace them with the love You have for me. Show me how to appreciate the amazing body that You have given me. Help me take better care of it.

the Holy Spirit
DWELLS INSIDE OF
your perfect,
COMPLETE BODY.

day sixteen

YOU ARE STRONG

I learned strength from so many people in my life, but I think I got it from my Mama. You see, when her brother was killed, I was a very little girl. I don't remember the initial years after it happened, but I grew up watching my Mom turn her grief, her pain, her sadness, and her loss into a ministry. She may not even call it that, but looking back, I see how God used the hardest thing in her life to bless people, counsel them, and write laws to protect people. She could have crawled into a hole for the rest of her life, and no one would have blamed her. But she didn't do that. She had a series of small choices that led her to the place God could use her. Everyday was a choice to move forward or retreat.

Strength looks different on everyone. Strength for some can look like simply making it out of bed every morning, getting out of the house, staying in a marriage, building a business from nothing, or fighting a disease. The depth of our strength is carved out in the moments when we have nothing physically, emotionally, or mentally to give, but we dig deep within our soul to find that our strength never actually came from us in the first place. Ephesians 6:10 commands us to be strong in the Lord, and the strength of His might. His might. Not yours. His might is where we draw our strength. We aren't fighting alone. We were never meant to.

I remind myself daily, sometimes hourly, that our struggle isn't against flesh and blood. When we are at odds with people, it is spiritual. There are spirits at work to cause dissension and strife, so it is our job to rely entirely on God's strength in those moments. When you feel weak and tired, remind yourself that your spirit is on the front lines all the time. 1 Peter 5:8 tells us that your adversary, the devil, prowls around like a roaring lion, seeking someone to devour. Your adversary. He is trying to defeat you. He is, literally, sneaking around, looking for ways to obliterate you. Know why? Because you are a threat. You are his adversary. The strength that you pull from God defeats him, so he is going to try to beat you to it.

How is he going to try and defeat you? Ever get mad at your kids and blow up? Ever want to strangle your husband? Ever get into a fight with a girlfriend? Ever give up on a project that you know you are meant to do? Ever let doubt and fear become your constant looped tape in your brain? Ever see a cute guy and you let your mind wander to what if's? Ever think that if you could just make it all stop that you wouldn't hurt anymore? You see, he's a snake. Literally and figuratively. He's not going to hand you a big, fat sin. No, girl, he is going to sneak little things in so that you comprise a belief or two. Those will compound and become a couple more beliefs. Soon, you will find yourself neck-deep in sin, unaware of the split-second when it all started to unravel.

Depressed? You shouldn't be. We know his tactics. We have his number. He is a one-trick pony, and we have the Spirit Who raised Christ from the dead living inside of us. You want to talk about strength? There is no greater power in the world than that, and girl, it is inside of you. So, yes, you are strong because that strength is in you, anytime you need it. And let me tell you, you're going to need it each and every moment.

You are strong. You are not alone. You are not on the front lines alone. You have the power of God living inside of you, fighting for you and with you. And spoiler alert: the good Guy wins at the end of the story. The bad guy? It's going to get a whole lot uglier for that piece.

...be strong in the Lord, and the strength of His might.
Ephesians 6:10 ESV

You

ARE STRONG.

You

ARE NOT ALONE.

Stop right where you are. I can hear the doubt in your head. You are strong. You have power. You are not fighting this battle alone.

Do you believe that God can give you the strength that you need to fight big and small battles?

Release the belief that you are the exception to this rule and that you are weak, and replace it with the truth that the Spirit Who raised Christ from the dead lives inside of you. The greatest power in the world lives in your spirit. Own it, rock it, use it.

———————

God, I can't do hard things without You. Thank You for giving me such immense power and strength. Thank You for not leaving my side in the battles. Remind me to lean into Your strength when I feel weak and defeated. Remind me that I'm on the winning team.

day seventeen

YOU HAVE PURPOSE

I know most of us wouldn't dare put pants on if we really don't have to, but have you walked into a bookstore lately? Or maybe, if you're like me, your pantless shopping choice is Amazon. Have you perused the self-help section? Have you seen the tens of thousands of titles that all promise some kind of freedom from the lies we are living in?

Girl, that is a problem. When the self-help section begins to overtake a bookstore, it is time for a shift in our culture. We have become so entirely consumed by our daddy issues, our eating disorders, our anxiety and depression, our abandonment issues, and every other disorder out there that we have entirely lost our sense of worth. We have resolved ourselves to live with a negative title because those "self-help" books tell us to embrace who we really are. Do not shy away from what's broken.

Not only are we told to embrace, but we are also told that

we don't need to change or work through these things. We are told to not apologize for who we are - that's just the way God made us. All throughout Scripture, God uses situations to sharpen His people, to smooth out the disorders and the issues. He doesn't want us to settle for "good enough." Proverbs 13:24 tells us that our choices have consequences, and they aren't a bad thing.

In 1 Peter 2, Peter is writing a letter to the churches in Asia, and he's casting God's vision to them. They are going to be the beginning of the Roman Catholic church. They are the stones, pillars, and foundation by which the Catholic church is built. They have a big freaking job to do as key players in history. He's also promising that they will have issues - daddy issues, anxiety and depression, martyrdom, hatred. These pillars aren't any different from you and I - they just wore more tunics and sandals than we do. Oh, and they didn't have Starbucks.

Peter is giving them fair warning that they are going to face hard times and they are going to struggle, but then, he says, that it doesn't matter because they are a chosen generation, a royal priesthood, a holy nation, and God's special treasure. Do you think they had time to sit around, reading self-help books?

Hear my heart: I am not saying that these are not valid hurts and heartbreaks because they are. However, this is not how God wants you to live. He wants you to live complete and whole through Him because you have such a calling on your life that requires you to push through the mud and muck.

You, precious one, are picked out of your generation to change your generation, to be the beginning of a royal line of Christ-followers, and are set apart to fulfill your holy calling. You have so much work to do! the other side of trials - He brought David to a place greater than David could imagine.

I can promise you this: the enemy will use every tactic to try and mess with you as you embrace your role. Phone calls will come in that knock the wind out of you, people will come out of the woodwork to say something nasty and hurtful about you, you and your spouse will fight, your relationships will all be tested because when you are working on God's kingdom, you have now become a threat to the prince of darkness. His agenda includes ruining lives one whisper at a time.

You are destined for greatness. You do not have to sit back and accept whatever life throws at you. You have the Spirit who raised Jesus to life living in you. You have a calling on your life so huge that there's no time to waste on feeling defeated. Get going, girl!

But you are a chosen people, a royal priesthood, a holy nation, God's special possession, that you may declare the praises of him who called you out of darkness into his wonderful light.
1 Peter 2:9 NIV

Do you know that your faith has the power to impact future generations? That you could be the reason your family accepts Christ and goes to heaven with you?

Are you making that impact now?

Have you allowed God to sharpen you for this greater purpose?

Release the belief that your faith isn't big enough to make an impact, and replace it with who you really are: a chosen woman, a royal priesthood, and a holy nation.

Jesus, I ask You to use me. Use my faith to lead my family, my friends, and the people around me to You. Give me the strength to stand up to distractions so that I can focus on You and Your plan for my life. Dig in deep and uproot the hurts that have taken up residence in my heart. Give me comfort during those times, and peace in knowing that they won't last. Thank You for making me complete in You.

You

ARE

destined

FOR

greatness.

day eighteen

YOU ARE AN OVERCOMER

The month before I got pregnant with the twins I was not on speaking terms with God. He may have been speaking to me, but I was tired of listening. My body was getting back on track after my fifth miscarriage, I weighed the lowest I'd ever weighed thanks to a second battle with an eating disorder, and I began having such horrible anxiety that I was sent to a neurologist for tingling in my extremities. I could barely leave my house because my fears had completely taken over.

I sunk deep into my new reality: failure. I was supposed to be able to have a babies as a woman. It was what my body was designed to do, and instead, my body wouldn't sustain a pregnancy. My body was failing me, and I was failing as a woman. Not only that, but I prayed constantly that God would take away my desire for more kids. If this was my reality, then why would my heart ache constantly to fill our home with babies? It was excruciating.

I knew every empowering scripture, I knew what to say when people asked about keeping the faith, but I was angry, hurt, and let down. I would announce to friends and family that month that it was the last month for conception. I couldn't take anymore "trying" or miscarriages. Win, lose, or draw we would try one last time for a baby, and then, it was time to move on.

Wouldn't you know that the Great Comedian had planned a twin pregnancy for me. The shock was real, the fear was real, and the emotions were real. I was on bed rest by 13 weeks, in labor at 27 weeks, hospital bed rest for 6 weeks, and finally, delivered twin boys at just past 35 weeks. I was Superwoman. The body that I had dishonored and abused, had carried twin babies to term. I was no longer a failure - I was an overcomer.

I relate so much to David. David has this hot and cold, Ross & Rachel-type relationship with God. I relate to that so well. The Psalms are his bipolar love affair with His God, and it's so incredible that God picked this man to be the author of so many beautiful love letters. You see, all throughout David's life, he battled with sin and pride and just really crappy circumstances. But the beauty is that even when he is being tested, being refined, getting trampled on, God always brought him to a place of abundance. Abundance. God didn't just get him to the other side of trials - He brought David to a greater place than he could ever imagine.

I read Psalm 66 and I am brought to tears even today. God tested me; He refined me like silver. He brought me into prison and laid burdens so heavy on my back. He let people ride over my head; I went through fire and water, and He brought me to a place of abundance. What I couldn't see then that I can see now is that God used that time in my life for so much more than pain and suffering. He used that time to iron some junk out that I was holding onto. He uses it now to breathe life into other women who are suffering the same losses. Not to mention, I have 2 beautiful sons that are worth every moment I went through.

God will always make your story come full circle. You are promised an uphill battle here on earth, but His Word promises you abundance. Your pain and suffering will not be for nothing. You're in the trenches now, sweetheart, but soon, you will wake up and take a deep breath. Abundance is on the other side of this hill. He promises you that.

As I write this, my teenie, tiny preemies just turned 4-years-old, and we celebrated with a superhero birthday party. Seems entirely fitting since their Mama is an over-coming superhero herself.

———————

For you, God, tested us; you refined us like silver. You brought us into prison and laid burdens on our backs. You let people ride over our heads; we went through fire and water, but you brought us to a place of abundance.
Psalm 66:10-12 NIV

Are you in the trenches, fighting to keep your head above water?

Are you in a season of harvest? Can you look back on the desert and see purpose?

Release the lie that you are defeated and that life will overtake you, and replace it with the truth that the Spirit of God Who has overcome the world lives inside of you. The power of God is inside of you just waiting to be used.

God, thank You for taking my circumstances and using them to teach me. I ask that you bring my story full circle. Use my battles to teach others. Thank You for the promise of abundance on the other sides of my trials. Thank You that you are faithful to complete the good work You began in me.

Abundance

IS ON THE

other side

OF THIS

hill.

day nineteen

YOU ARE A CONQUEROR

What's the hardest thing you have ever faced in your life? Can you recall to memory the agony that knocked the wind out of you? Can you recall the physical pain your body felt? Did you beg God to take that cup from you? Did you barter with Him?

I have had bad things happen, even tragic things happen in my life, but I won't sit here and tell you my stories. Each of us has deep, soul-shaking pain that we have endured, some deeper and more awful than others. I know people who have lost spouses and children and parents. Their pain rocks them to the core, making it nearly impossible to breathe some days.

What I have witnessed as an outsider of those tragedies is the triumph of the human spirit. I have seen men and women get up out of the fog of grief and, not only function, but soar. I have seen the greatest ministries and testimonies come from deep within the recesses of those broken hearts. That is not a coincidence. 1 Corinthians 15:57 tells us that God gives us victory. When the worst, most unthinkable tragedy happens, we have the the Spirit of the Living God inside of us to get us up, out of bed, and to be victorious in our lives.

Paul addresses earthly suffering in Romans 8. He promises that we will go through tragedy and pain here. You are not guaranteed an easy life. What we get to help us through it is the Holy Spirit (John 16:7). He tells us that even when our spirits are utterly destroyed, the Spirit prays for us when we don't have the strength to utter a word. Sometimes the tears and the groans are all we can muster, so the Spirit intercedes to the Father for us. So, yes, you will suffer tragedy, but you don't stay there. Your heart doesn't remain in that broken state. Verse 37 tells us that we are more than conquerors because we have the King on our side.

This tells me that we are made to thrive. We are made to be overcomers, squaring off our shoulders, jaw set, and heading into the storm, knowing we are going to come out of it better than before. While my stories of miscarriage pale in comparison to some of the grief I know others have experienced, I have seen how God has taken my deepest, soul-crushing hurts and used them to speak life and love over other women. I could not see any of that while I was in the trenches. Tragedy and loss will never leave, but God can use them. There will be others in your life who will suffer similar pain, and God will be able to use you to come alongside them in their deepest moments of grief.

On this side of heaven, loss and death make no sense. There will never be a good enough reason for our loved ones to be taken from us suddenly. I do believe that when we dig deep and let God begin to heal our hearts that He can use our biggest heartbreaks to be a light in a very dark world. We can be His vessels if we will let Him use us. Even in the midst of great tragedy, there will always be light.

Dear one, you may be reading this thinking, "she doesn't know the kind of loss I've endured." And you would be right. I do not. Some of your pains and hurts and heartbreaks are so soul-shattering that I cannot begin to understand your pain. But oh, love, your Maker knows. He grieves with you. If you think back to that moment and you ask your Father to show you where He was in the moment, I guarantee you would see Him right next to you in your mind's eye. But you are more than a conqueror. This tragedy will not consume you. This hurt will not overcome you. You have the Spirit Who raised Christ from the dead living inside of you. You are stronger than you think.

———————

In all these things we are more than conquerors through him who loved us.
Romans 8:37 NIV

———————

Can you pinpoint your greatest loss? Maybe you're in the midst of it now.

Have you seen how you can be used even in loss? Has God used your loss to be a light to others yet?

Have you looked for a way to be used?

Release the lie that your losses will defeat you, and replace it with the truth that you are the head and not the tail, more than a conqueror, and that Your God is mighty to save you in the worst trials.

I know You can relate to me because You suffered the greatest loss when You sent Your Son to die for me. Thank You that You are acompassionate God Who understands my hurts and losses. I cling to the truth that You have me in the palm of Your hand, and that Your plan for me is not to be defeated, but to be raised up. I accept and believe Your Word.

You
ARE
stronger
THAN
you think.

day twenty

YOU ARE WONDERFUL

Do you know when I do the biggest battles? You guessed it. Once a month. For a week. Clutching a pint of Cookies 'n' Cream. Do you get trapped in your head? Do you feel the absolute worst about yourself? If you are nodding in agreement, grab your ice cream, and let's have a good cry together.

Without making calendar notes, I can see my cycle coming a mile away. Like clockwork, two days in advance, I begin to get very weepy. Like, Nicholas-Sparks-movie-level weeping. Kindness makes me cry, sadness makes me cry, commercials make me cry. All of it. Good or bad, crying.

Have you ever stood in the mirror and just looked over your body? Have you stood there, picking each lump and bump apart, willing your thighs to let some air between, wishing your chest wasn't pointing so far south, or hissing at the stretch marks that litter your stomach and hips? You're not alone. I wish that I could tell you that writing this study means that I have mastered positive body image, but it's just not the case.

Have you ever seen leaked magazine images of celebrities? Have you seen how every inch of their body is nipped and tucked and airbrushed to "perfection?" Girl, it's because it's not real. What you are wishing you could look like is not real. The bodies that you see on the cover of magazines are not real. They are made on a computer screen. The lie you are believing that you should look a certain way damages every part of your being. Your mind is fixated on what's unattainable, you covet in your heart, you abuse your body to force it to look a certain way, you speak negativity over yourself.

According to The American Society of Plastic Surgeons, 17.5 million cosmetic procedures took place in 2017. In that same study, the ASPS reported that in 2016, Americans spent $16 billion on cosmetic surgery. To attain something that isn't humanly possible. To fit a society's standards. To feel better about ourselves.

Dear one, you don't need it. You are so perfect exactly how your Creator made you. Those claw marks on your stomach? They were earned while you carried around a giant baby for 9 months. Those thighs that touch? Hey, I bet you haven't dropped your cell phone in the toilet! The lines on your face? They tell me that you are a lot of fun to be around because you must laugh a lot. And that badonkadonk? At least your pants will always stay up.

You were made by a perfect God Who tells us in Psalm 139 that we are fearfully and wonderfully made. I have recited it a million times, but it wasn't until I opened my commentary to unpack this verse that I grasped its wonder. What David is saying by fearfully is that we are a sight to behold, a creation to stand in awe of. We are a magnificent creation to behold. You are marvelous. Your body is so intricate and complex that it is awe-inspiring.

I'll be honest this lie is going to be tough to release, but it's something that you can practice on a daily basis. The act of speaking life over your body will feel awkward at first, but soon, you will learn to appreciate the power you wield over your mind. In turn, those words are going to begin blooming in your heart, and you will not only say it, but you will believe it.

For you formed my inward parts; you knitted me together in my mother's womb. I praise you, for I am fearfully and wonderfully made. Wonderful are your works; my soul knows it very well.
Psalm 139:13-14 ESV

Do you believe that you are wonderful? Do you stand in awe of what you are able to do?

Release the lie that you are not enough, as well as the lies that our world has whispered in your ear. Replace those lies with the truth that you are fearfully and wonderfully made, and that every square inch of you was handcrafted by your Creator.

Father, thank You for my imperfections and my flaws. Thank You for creating me in Your perfect image. My body has done so many amazings things that only a God Who has a vast imagination could have created. Forgive me for the times that I have wanted to alter it in any way. From here on out, help me appreciate all of my lumps and bumps instead of wishing I looked like an airbrushed model.

You

ARE

marvelous.

day twenty-one

YOU ARE APPOINTED

One of the best ways I lost my identity was when I became a mom. The second those two pink lines popped up on the stick, I was completely enraptured in baby clothes, baby blankets, baby shoes, baby everything. My entire world became about preparing for this new little life. I didn't care about anything else. The day I found out that I was having a girl, I began painting her room. I had the crib and dresser picked out the next day. Everything about having a baby had completely consumed me, and I was only too happy to give in.

When my daughter was born, I did little else besides stare at her. She was a very easy baby, sleeping 8 hours a night beginning at 4 days old. I'll never forget the sheer panic when she was sleeping so soundly. This wasn't supposed to happen! And believe me, it didn't once the boys were born.

Life continued on in a pattern of nursing, changing, sleeping, nursing, changing, sleeping. The monotony of life with an infant settled in, and to be honest, I was bored. My house was clean because it was just the two of us. I didn't have any hobbies or interests that were begging for my time.

I was a mom. I had fully embraced dry shampoo, sweat pants, and nursing tanks that were usually covered in spit up. I wasn't suffering from postpartum depression, but I was definitely in the throes of postpartum loss of identity. In an effort to regain some of that, I started going out and trying different things. I made an effort to go meet other moms, to get into Bible studies, to try new things like photography. I knew that deep inside of me, God had given me a drive - I just hadn't figured out what that was.

You have goals and dreams and visions for your life because God instilled those specifics into your heart. Each of us is so vastly different, and because of that the call on your life is going to look entirely different from mine. John 15:16 tells us that God chose each of us to make a specific impact on the world that only we can make. For a lot of you reading this, part of your impact in the world will be to embrace your season of motherhood and turn those babies into amazing humans who will go out and change the world. For a lot of us, our sphere of influence is going to be where we impact the world for good. The friends and family that surround you are the ones that you are going to change with your heart and your love for Christ. And then for some, you will go on to preach to people from a stage. You will share insights and wisdom that the Lord has given you to empower others to be a light in their world.

You are not one thing. You are not only a mom. You are not only a business owner. You are not only an employee. You are not only a doctor or nurse. You are not only a wife. You are not only a daughter. You are a million different things, and God gives you the ability to use the gifts and talents you have to go reach people who need you. I can't be what your friends need. You can't be what my friends need. We can only do what God has laid before us, but we can do it so well. And He tells you that He won't leave you hanging! He will complete the good work He started in you.

You have greatness in you. I know that because the Bible says so. You have specific tasks laid out before you that only you can do for the kingdom of God. You are going to make waves, change lives, and make your Daddy proud. Man, you're amazing!

You did not choose me, but I chose you and appointed you so that you might go and bear fruit—fruit that will last—and so that whatever you ask in my name the Father will give you.
John 15:16 NIV

What dreams has God given you?

Are you actively pursuing them?

Release the lie that you aren't made to be so many amazing things, and replace it with the truth that you are appointed to bear fruit in your own life and the lives of others.

You chose me and appointed me for a specific task. A lot of times, I feel like I can't do it. Thank You for promising to give me whatever I need to bear fruit. Remind me of Your perfection when my weakness is overtaking me. Remind me that I can rest in Your arms when the weight of the world is on me.

He will

COMPLETE

the good work

HE STARTED

in you.

day twenty-two

YOU ARE WORTH IT

When I was in high school, I had a teacher incorrectly share that at some point in our lives, God would throw His hands up, and walk away from us. I do not remember the circumstances of that class, but I can guarantee that that teacher was at his wits' end with a roomful of teenagers.

Unfortunately, whatever else was said that day, these are the only words that sank in. I walked around the rest of the day feeling like a complete and total loser. I was screwed. I was a sassy teenager, so clearly, my eternal life was now in jeopardy. Where was the God Who had sent His Son to die for my sins? I assumed it meant that that portion of grace hadn't been enough to cover the pile of sins that I had committed.

I wish I could say that I was strong enough in my faith and understanding of the Bible that I didn't let that one day make an impact on my life, but that's just not the case. That lie followed me around for a long time, and really confused my relationship with God. I was back to knowing the God of the Old Testament Who smote people and pillar-of-salted an obnoxious woman. I even joked with people that the pillar of salt thing was long overdue, and likely, I was the next candidate. I make jokes when I'm uncomfortable.

Not too many years ago, I heard someone speak on the matter of grace and the death of Jesus. It was a teaching I'd heard many times over, but this was the one that finally pierced my heart. He read 2 Corinthians 2:19: "My grace is sufficient for you, for my power is made perfect in weakness. Therefore I will boast all the more gladly about my weaknesses, so that Christ's power may rest on me." Grace covers our sin - His grace was enough for me. The speaker went on to say that when we don't accept the work of the cross, we are saying that Christ's death wasn't enough to cover our sins. Whoa!

It was all coming into focus. His death, His blood shed, His grace were all enough. In my finite, human mind, it made no sense. It couldn't be. I wasn't worth that kind of sacrifice. I was too much and not enough for His sacrifice to cover me. I had believed for so long that I was the exception to the rule, but all God was asking me to do was to accept it. Romans 5:6 goes on to tell me that even in my worst, most ugly sin, He died for me. The worst things I could ever do, and I'm still worth it.

I am worth it. *You* are worth it. It's not a pass to live like an animal, but it's a gift that we get to accept daily, even when we don't deserve it. Your job isn't to understand it - your job is to graciously accept the free gift you have been given and never look back. If that gift doesn't compel you to fall deeply in love with your Creator, then I don't know what will.

You may have heard (or believe) that you aren't worth it, but John 3:16 negates that lie. He loved you so stinkin' much that He died for you so that we can be a family together forever. Accept it. You are worth it. He knows it, I know it. It's time for you to let that truth take root in your heart and let it grow wildly.

You see, at just the right time, when we were still powerless, Christ died for the ungodly.
Romans 5:6 NIV

Do you believe that you are worth it? Do you believe that if it had just been you, Christ still would have died just for you?

Release the lie that you aren't worthy of Christ's love and death, and replace it with the truth of His sacrifice for you because of His love for you.

Jesus, I don't deserve it, but I accept it. Show me daily that I am worth it. Show me daily that You think of me. Show me daily that I am enough because You made me enough. Your grace is enough and I accept it today and everyday. Thank You, Jesus.

You

ARE

worth it.

day twenty-three

YOU ARE A CO-HEIR

I grew up in southern California pretty close to the beach. I had my own room, lived in a safe, nice neighborhood, and we had everything we needed and a lot of things we wanted. My Mom's family was all in the same area, so my sister and I spent most of our childhood with our extended family. My Mom came from a large family, so we had a lot of cousins to play with as kids.

When we were little, my grandparents lived in a trailer park. The family loving called their trailer "the tin can." As kids, we didn't care. We played hide and seek between the lemon trees, hid behind the sun porch after stealing the lemon drops that Grandma always had in glass candy dishes, and laid on the blue carpet under the swamp cooler when the desert sun became too hot to endure. At Christmas, all 16 of us would squeeze into the trailer for our traditional Mexican food Christmas Eve dinner, careful to navigate the pile of presents that stretched the entire length of the living room.

We sat on floral couches with our plates balanced on our laps, waited in line for our turn in the one bathroom, and soon began the flurry of ripping presents open. In that moment, we were all just together. There was no tin can, no trailer park address - just pure joy. Being there each Christmas, packed in with my family, are some of my favorite memories.

As an adult with kids of my own, I see so much value in the traditions that we create and eventually pass on to our children. The setting isn't the point - the value in those moments is. The inheritance that I get to take away from my time in that home is the inheritance that matters. The joy and love (and sarcasm) is what I feel when I think back to those Christmases.

Romans 8:17 tells us that if we are children of God then we are co-heirs to the inheritance of the kingdom of God. I believe that we will get to live together with Christ, but I know that it also means that there is so much more than mansions and jewels in heaven. Jesus made the decision to give up His life so that we might share His inheritance with Him. His inheritance is far beyond the Kingdom of God, but is also fullness of joy, permanent adoption, and union with God. Our inheritance is in sharing those moments that only a family can share together. Our inheritance is so much more than things - it's wholeness and togetherness.

In my mind, eternity in heaven looks like those Christmas Eve celebrations as a child. We are elbow to elbow, balancing plates on laps, snorting enchiladas, and it's just complete and total chaos, but the joy is overwhelming. The sense of wholeness and acceptance permeates the walls, and we are a family. We are all flawed and weird and broken, but we are a family.

So, I'll save you a seat up there. Do you like sour cream on your enchiladas, co-heir?

Now if we are children, then we are heirs—heirs of God and co-heirs with Christ, if indeed we share in his sufferings in order that we may also share in his glory.
Romans 8:17 NIV

What inheritance do you want to leave behind? Is it things or traditions, character, and love?

Release the lie that you don't deserve your inheritance, and replace it with the truth that you are a co-heir with Jesus. You are going to share in that amazing glory!

God, it's so hard to believe that I get to inherit the kingdom with You. Thank You for loving me so much that You want to make me a permanent family member. Thank You for giving me the paper plates and not the fancy China, and for making me one of Your kids. I can't wait to give You a bear hug.

We
ARE ALL
flawed
AND WEIRD
and broken,
BUT WE ARE
a family.

day twenty-four

YOU ARE FORGIVEN

Have you ever peeled apart an onion layer by layer? The outer part is thin and easily torn apart. Each layer gets a little tighter, more hidden, and stronger. Onions can make your eyes water, and are even tough to swallow raw, but when you cut just a small amount or cook the onion, you find that it's easier to stomach and it's actually really good for you. Onions are packed with nutrients, and fun fact, are helpful in fighting osteoporosis.

Yeah, this is a weird way to start this day, but stick with me!

Think of a time when you've done something to hurt someone you love and care about. Those initial moments when they find out is just the surface - the shell has torn away and you both are reeling with what was done.

In my life, I have made some very bad mistakes with people that I loved very much. I have let pride, jealousy, anger, passion, and hurt take root, and pull me away from the relationship. I have been in situations where, even though I was right, my approach was wrong. And in those instances, I have had to forgive myself and forgive that person. Each of those moments of forgiveness is peeling back another layer of forgiveness and releasing.

Have you ever forgiven and forgotten, only to find that, 6 months later, you are thrust into those same thoughts and feelings? Have you ever believed that you have peeled back all of those layers, but realize that the roots are still there? I think so much of this depends on our spiritual maturity at different stages in life. You will find that you might repeat the same patterns of hurt and unforgiveness for a while, but then, move to a deeper level of understanding where you can forgive yet again.

Forgiveness is a big deal in the Bible. Because of the gift of the cross, we are forgiven. Our debt has been paid, and we stand totally forgiven before our Lord. Psalm 103:10-14 tells us that He doesn't see our sins - He has removed them so far from His memory that they are as far as the east is from the west. It's a done deal, girl. You are forgiven.

So, why does the Bible hit so hard on us forgiving others? The Word says that we need to forgive the people who have wronged us so that God can forgive us. What good does it do us to harbor bitterness, resentment, anger, and unforgiveness? It doesn't. You know people in your life who are unable to forgive, and it shows on their outward appearance. God is telling you, for your own physical, spiritual, and mental health to forgive the people in your life who have hurt you. That release causes our hearts and minds to settle, and God forgives you. Simple as that.

I look back at my damaged relationships like those onion layers. At different points in my life, God has decided it was time to peel back another layer and deal with any hurt or unforgiveness still harbored in my heart. Delving deeper into these layers is a form of therapy between us and God, as He uses our obedience to mold us into more effective vessels of His Word. These times are hard, but they can be so cathartic and rewarding if we allow God to help us release these broken relationships layer by layer.

For if you forgive others their trespasses, your heavenly Father will also forgive you.
Matthew 6:14 NIV

Do you have people in your life you need to forgive? Do you need to do it more than once?

Do you truly believe that you have been forgiven, and are now blameless before God?

Release the lie that you are not forgiven, and replace it with the simple truth that God has forgiven you once and for all.

God, forgive me for the times I have been unforgiving. Forgive me for believing that I am more deserving of grace than a friend. I release any unforgiveness or bitterness to You, and ask You to fill me with grace, love, and mercy. Help me to forgive freely and often.

It's a
DONE DEAL,
girl.
YOU ARE
forgiven.

day twenty-five

YOU LACK NOTHING

I don't like to ask for help. I am a strong, self-sufficient woman who only sometimes has blonde moments. I carried fussy twins for 7 months, I can change a tire, and can make the fluffiest, lightest macarons this side of the Mississippi. If there is a tutorial for it, I will watch it and replicate it. I am creative, handy, and stubborn. I decide on a project and I will complete it.

If I have to ask for help, it's a quiet, "hey, would you possibly mind maybe helping me a little?" I pride myself on being able to accomplish tasks, and getting stuck is only further proof that I am, indeed, human.

When my second son was born, he emerged grumpy and annoyed that he had been taken from my body. He was also not breathing on his own. I was wheeled in to see my boys about an hour after my c-section, only to find them hooked up to every machine imaginable to help them gain weight, breathe, and just stay alive. I had failed. That room in the NICU was proof that I had failed. I couldn't keep them in long enough for them to breathe on their own, my body had been so touchy during my entire pregnancy. I wasn't enough for my children.

Motherhood is the ultimate accuser of failure. Your kid eats dog poop (true story), you lock them inside the house alone (also, a true story), and they swallow pennies and need Heimlich-ed (yep, that's true too). There is nothing harder than getting up every single day to kids who need you to be everything to them when you feel entirely depleted before your eyelids even flutter open.

It is impossible to survive parenthood without help. You are not made to be everything to everyone. You are made to rely on a God Who wants to help lift your head off your pillow, grab the strongest cup of coffee imaginable, and attack each day. Every single day is a marathon. You are waking up to children yelling, bills piling up, leaking toilets, grumpy spouses, and a to-do list longer than your arm.

James 1 tells us that these moments in your life are molding you and shaping you. You're becoming the best version of yourself. God tells us that when we are running our marathons to tag Him in, ask Him for what you need, and He will give it to you. He goes on to tell us that He isn't judging us or thumbing His nose at us, but He's saying, "girl, what do you need? How can I help?"

Everything that you need to make it to the finish line is

available to you if you just ask. Don't be stubborn like me - ask Him for what you need and He is faithful to give it to you. Take Him up on the offer. Everything that you need is in His wheelhouse and He's generous.

May your coffee be strong, and may your toddlers be quiet. But not too quiet because that means they are getting into trouble.

Let perseverance finish its work so that you may be mature and complete, not lacking anything. If any of you lacks wisdom, you should ask God, who gives generously to all without finding fault, and it will be given to you.
James 1:4-5 NIV

Do you feel depleted before you even get out of bed?

Did you know that God has everything you need to be the very best version of yourself each and every day?

Release the lie that you aren't enough and are unequipped to finish your race, and replace that lie with the truth that God gives you everything you need to complete the task He has given you.

Father, I need You. I need Your help to make it through each day. I come up short each day, so I need You to step in and give me the tools I need to run this race. Thank You for making us reliant on You, so that we need to be in constant communion with You. I trust You and I believe that You will give me everything I need. Help me to be the best version of myself I can be.

Ask Him

FOR WHAT

you need,

AND HE WILL

give

IT TO YOU.

day twenty-six

YOU ARE NEVER ALONE

I have struggled on and off with anxiety since I was 17-years-old. I remember walking into the doctor's office for the first time. My palms were sweaty, my heart was beating out of chest, and the blood rushing in my ears was deafening.

I was diagnosed with anxiety disorder. I was told that I would deal with anxiety for the rest of my life because of the way my brain was wired, and I settled into that. It was both comforting and irritating. Comforting because I wasn't crazy, and irritating because I didn't want to live like this for the rest of my life. I was handed a prescription and sent on my merry way.

Ironically, with the prescription on the passenger seat of my car, I sat in a gas station parking lot and had the biggest anxiety attack I'd ever experienced. My arms and legs started to go numb. I was definitely dying. This was it. No one else could possibly understand what I was thinking or feeling. The waves of panic washed over me again and again for about twenty minutes.

I was alone, in a parking lot, believing that I would never be free of this prison I was in. My boyfriend didn't understand me, my friends didn't understand, and I certainly didn't understand what I had done to be served this punishment. I was all alone inside of my own head, and it was consuming me.

I think one of the biggest lies that our enemy tries to get us to believe is that we are alone. Think about it. How many times a day do you think, "why me? I'm the only one who has to deal with _____." No one knows how embarrassing our families truly are, no one else has kids who are out of control, no one else struggles with food issues, no one knows what it's like to suffer from debilitating anxiety or depression, no one could possibly understand the hurt and pain that I have been through. Those thoughts can isolate you and make you an island.

When we begin to believe the lies that no one can understand us or commiserate with us, it is easy to pull away and shut our emotions down. The best thing that your enemy can do is get you alone and silent because then you are rendered completely ineffective. Isolated and quiet changes nothing and no one, yourself included.

But what happens when you open up? What happens when a small light is shed in darkness? What happens when you tell your fears to shove it? You become powerful, effective, and a light. You become someone who helps others when they begin to share their struggles with you.

When I was brave enough to share what I was feeling, I found out that so many women (and some men) were dealing with the same type of anxiety that I was. We were all clammy and short of breath together, and we had no idea. When I decided I was no longer ashamed, the weight I'd been carrying suddenly seemed lighter.

And while I can't give you a good enough explanation as to why we struggle with anxiety and depression while we're here, I believe that we can use it to minister to other people who are in the throes of their own battle. I promise that you will find that the very thing you're struggling is something that many thousands are struggling with as well.

In the book of Joshua, God is speaking to Joshua about His plans for Joshua's life. Moses has just died, and now, Joshua is taking up his torch. He has a big task ahead of him, and I'm betting his heart was racing and his hands were drenched in sweat. But God assures him in verse 5 - *"hey, I was tight with Moses and I'm going to be tight with you. I promise not to ever leave you. We're going to do this together."*

Zephaniah prophesied over a repentant Israel and tells them in chapter 3, verse 7 *"The Lord your God is with you, the Mighty Warrior who saves. He will take great delight in you; in his love he will no longer rebuke you, but will rejoice over you with singing."*

All throughout scripture, Christ is called Emmanuel, God with us. Plus, before Jesus' death, He tells His disciples that He's about to leave, but He's sending a Helper to be with us always.

You just aren't alone. You can't be because your God is with you wherever you go. Your Helper is just a whisper away. When the darkness feels consuming, cry out to the Lord because He's right there with you. And when you're ready, tell friends you trust what you're dealing with. Odds are that at least one of them can empathize because they too have felt the way you do.

So, go start your own anxiety society. They're waiting to be sweaty and anxious with you.

No one will be able to stand against you all the days of your life. As I was with Moses, so I will be with you; I will never leave you nor forsake you.
Joshua 1:5 NIV

Do you feel like no understands the struggle you're facing? Because of that belief, do you feel isolated and alone?

135

Release the lie that you are alone and that no one could possibly understand what you're going through, and replace it with the truth that your Helper is only a breath away.

God, I feel so alone. I feel like no one understands or struggles the way I do, but I know that it isn't true. I know that you created us for community, and that means that there are lots of other people out there who will understand me. Show me who they are. Holy Spirit, remind me when I feel alone that You are always with me. Thank You for not abandoning me in my despair. Thank You for being my constant Helper.

You

JUST AREN'T

alone.

day twenty-seven

YOU ARE
CHOSEN AND PRECIOUS

If you have kids, you love each of them the same amount, but you love them differently. I have 3 kids who are all very different. They have similarities about them, but they are very much their own person.

My daughter, Maddie, is a leader. She's smart, she's funny, she's charismatic, she's bold, she's loud, she's compassionate and empathetic, she's sunshine with a little hurricane, she's unabashedly herself. She loves people, hates to be alone, likes her space, but with someone in the room, loves without reserve, and is happy when everyone around her is happy.

My son, Jax, is strong. He's eloquent, well-spoken, methodical, pensive, quiet, thoughtful, reserved, shy, kind, goofy, and a little bit of a loner. He's comfortable around people he knows well, doesn't like strangers, entertains himself for hours at a time, but likes the comfort of being in the same room with one of us.

My son, Jett, is determined. He sits down and figures out whatever task is in front of him, no matter how long it takes. He's smart, he's funny, he's strong-willed, he's sensitive, and he's affectionate. Even though the boys are twins, they couldn't be more opposite in personality or stature.

All three of them have their own personality, strengths, and weaknesses. Each of them are irreplaceable and so precious. Together, the dynamic is lively and exciting and loving and crazy.

I think a lot about what things would be like without all of those miscarriages, but I don't get too far. I wouldn't have the three of them, and it wouldn't be the same. I would choose them over any other kids because they are exactly the kids I was meant to have. I may not have chosen to have twins, but I am so glad that God knew better.

I'm guessing you feel the same about your little ones. Yes, they make you crazy, you haven't slept through the night in years, and your uniform is a pair of sweatpants and t-shirt with a permanent mystery stain, but they are the kids you would choose if you'd been given a choice.

Your heavenly Father feels the same way about you. You might make Him want to pull His hair out, but He would choose you a thousand times over because you are precious to Him. The day that I stumbled across this verse in 1st Peter 2, my heart swelled. In the sight of God, I am chosen and precious. He chose me and He thinks I am precious. He thinks of me enough to feel so strongly about me. The love I have for my kids is just a fraction of the way God feels about me. He chose me for adoption, and thinks I have so much value that He wants to be with me and bless me.

You can't even begin to comprehend the thoughts He has about you. Psalm 139 tells us that He has so many that they would outnumbered the grains of sand on earth. He chose you. He chooses you. You are His precious daughter. You.

———————

As you come to him, a living stone rejected by men but in the sight of God chosen and precious.
1 Peter 2:4 ESV

———————

Do you believe that the God of the universe thinks that you are precious? Do you believe that He looked at you and picked you?

Release the lie that you don't belong and that you aren't handpicked, and replace it with the truth that He chose you and you are precious to Him.

Lord, being chosen by You is the greatest honor. Thank You for picking me, and for looking at me with such love and care. Thank You, Jesus, for thinking of me and for loving me so deeply that You made a way for us to be together forever. Thank You for showing me what true love is.

He chose

YOU.

He chooses

YOU.

day twenty-eight

YOU ARE BLESSED

As I came into adulthood, I began to hear more about this Proverbs 31 woman who, apparently, had her life together. She brings her husband good - not harm. She is creative and crafty. She sleeps for a few hours before getting up in the wee hours of the morning to prepare gourmet cuisines. She is good with her money. She is a philanthropist and loves people who need help. She makes her bed everyday. Her kids are all dressed well. She is strong and has impeccable character. She isn't anxious. She is wise and shares her wisdom. She has her household in check.

We get it! She's perfect. Her kids never yell at her and call her a poopy face. She only needs four hours of sleep, but she still looks like Cindy Crawford. She is the ultimate Pinterest mom. She doesn't have a closet full of shoes that were all impulses purchases. She is the ultimate Stepford wife. She's this elusive ideology that we wish we could be, but feel like we can't measure up to.

What gets missed so often in that passage is her most important characteristic: she fears her God. She stands in awe of Him. She adores Him.

We so often see this passage as a laundry list of to-do's that we can't possibly achieve each day of our busy lives, but we miss the point. These things fall into place when we stand in awe of our Creator. He begins to change our hearts and desires to finish the tasks that He puts before us. This traditional stay-at-home-mom has a to-do list that is only slightly different than ours. Some of us still stay at home with our kids all day, but so many of you are full-time employees and mamas. Your laundry list is no less important - it's just different.

This ruby of a woman honors her God with her work, her finances, her marriage, her parenting, and her character. God blesses her because of her love for Him and how she conducts herself. You may be wearing a pantsuit, but your work is just as honorable and praiseworthy. You are blessed because you work hard at what God has put before you.

You are blessed. When you feel like the laundry list is getting longer, begin saying your blessings out loud. When you step on a Lego, thank God for the kids that fill your home. When your husband leaves his dirty socks on the floor, thank God for the blessing of a good man. When the dishes are piled in the sink, thank God for food on your table. There are blessings all around you in everything you do.

You are blessed, girl. And if no one has said it lately, you are amazing at what you do.

Her children arise and call her blessed; her husband also, and he praises her: "Many women do noble things, but you surpass them all." Charm is deceptive, and beauty is fleeting; but a woman who fears the Lord is to be praised. Proverbs 31:28-30 NIV

Do you do the tasks before you because you are honoring God?

Has it crossed your mind that your work can be done for Him?

Do you know that you *are* the Proverbs 31 woman?

Release the lie that you don't measure up and you are missing the mark, and replace it with the truth that your tasks are what God has set before you to do well.

————————

Lord, forgive me for getting caught up in comparison. Forgive me for not valuing what I have been given. God, thank You that I am blessed. Thank You for giving me a passion and a purpose to fulfill. Thank You for my special gifts that only I have. I want to honor You with them.

If no one has
SAID IT LATELY,
you are
AMAZING AT
what you do.

day twenty-nine

YOU ARE SECURE

I loved roller coasters and thrill rides from a young age. I had no fear about flying through the air in a small cart or seat. I just trusted that I was safe. Even as a small kid, my Dad would take me on every roller coaster in the theme park. Eventually, he had to tap out, but I was still raring to go.

One of my favorite rides at Disneyland was called the Maliboomer. You sit in chair with a harness, and are shot up a 180-foot vertical tower at 40 miles an hour. It was absolutely terrifying and exhilarating. When Josh and I had our Disneyland passes, we would just stay on the ride on quiet days because no one was in line. I love the feeling of my stomach dropping, as you're seemingly flying through the air. While it was scary, I knew that the harness was going keep me locked into place and that there were safety precautions set up on the tower to keep us from flying off the top and into the air.

This world doesn't offer much in the way of security, but this is temporary. 2 Corinthians 1 tells us that our future is secure because when we received Christ, the Holy Spirit entered our hearts and was a seal on us. He is our ticket in. It is non-refundable, non-transferable. The guarantee that you have been given cannot be taken away, revoked, stolen, or denied. You can sit with us!

Precious one, I know that this life has had you on some crazy roller coasters, that, with nothing being guaranteed on earth, it has caused you stress and anxiety, and even despair. But relax because there is a place for you that is your own.

I know that so many of you reading this love Jesus, but if you are coming to the end of these 30 days and you haven't asked Him to seal you, you can do it in the quiet of your heart right now. There are no magic words - just a simple, Jesus, I believe You love me and died for me, and You are welcome into my heart and life forever. I want You to direct my steps because I have no clue what I'm doing. Show me how to love like You.

Or maybe you're in another camp. You've known Him for a while, but you've lost touch. Just acknowledge Him, tell Him you miss Him. He's there with you now. Because He's totally crazy about you.

Your future is rock solid. We have a seat for you. Will there be big assemblies where we all sit on bleachers? Or maybe a long farmhouse table where we pass the bread and wine? Either way, our tickets are valid. If I don't meet you down here, I'll give you a squeeze up there, sister.

...and who has also put his seal on us and given us his Spirit in our hearts as a guarantee.
2 Corinthians 1:22 ESV

Do you feel like you are floundering? Alone in this world?

Do you believe without a doubt that you are headed to the greatest place?

Release the lie that you are alone, and replace it with the truth of your secured eternity.

Jesus, thank You for my future. Thank You that I don't have to wonder or worry about where I am going. Give me peace when I feel anxious about my future, and remind me of the security only You can offer.

You

CAN

sit

WITH US!

day thirty

YOU ARE REDEFINED

You did it! I know this last month was tough. I forced you not only to look at the lies you've believed, but rip them out and replace them with the truth of God's Word.

Let me let you in a little secret: this isn't going to be completed and stamped today. This will be a battle in your mind throughout your life. You will have to get up each day and decide who is going to control your thoughts, whose words you are going to let take root, and what you are going to do with them. You will have setbacks, but you will have so many more victories, girl. When you actively renew your mind with the truth in God's Word, you are storing up the goodies for when the storms hit. You will be sharper and quicker to knock down words and lies that come at you.

I remember my lightbulb moment a few months ago about "daily bread." There are days that I don't make time to get into the Word, and I just go back to the old bread I'd read a few days back. When we pray, "give us this day, our daily bread," we are asking for a fresh word from God for each day we face. That bread that He gave me yesterday was for yesterday. The bread for tomorrow will be for tomorrow. Spending time, even if it's just 5 minutes a day, can make a huge difference in owning your identity. When you put the good stuff in, the good stuff is what flows out of you. You will be like a beautiful unicorn, spewing rainbows of God's goodness all over your friends.

Make today a stepping stone. Today is the day that you don't look back on your mistakes or your sins any longer, but instead step forward into the amazing story God has waiting for just you. Throw your arms wide open and accept the Truth. Declare it over your life. And when the storms start rolling in, you will be able to say and believe that you are new, very good, raised up, loved, not her, have a bright future, are called, seen, valuable, free, chosen, a child, comforted, saved, a temple of God, strong, have purpose, are an overcomer, a conqueror, wonderful, appointed, worth it, a co-heir, forgiven, lack nothing, never alone, chosen and precious, blessed, secure, and redefined.

What the world says about you is null and void because the true you is the you that God created. The world does not define you. You are now redefined by God.

Therefore, if anyone is in Christ, the new creation has come: The old has gone, the new is here!
2 Corinthians 5:17 NIV

How do you feel? Refreshed? Renewed? Redefined? Good! Repeat these affirmations to yourself. They are not made up - they come straight from the Word of God. Speak them over yourself daily, and I promise, it will become a habit. You will begin to accept and believe all of the good things that you were made to be.

———

Lord, we made it! Thank You for showing me truths about who I really am. I ask You to help me walk these out every single day. Thank You for redefining me.

You

ARE NOW

redefined

BY GOD.